A Trail Of Ecstasy

21 shades of bloom & gloom

Sakshi Singh

BookLeaf Publishing

India | USA | UK

Copyright @ Sakshi Singh
All Rights Reserved.

This book has been self-published with all reasonable efforts taken to make the material error-free by the author. No part of this book shall be used, reproduced in any manner whatsoever without written permission from the author, except in the case of brief quotations embodied in critical articles and reviews.

The Author of this book is solely responsible and liable for its content including but not limited to the views, representations, descriptions, statements, information, opinions, and references ["Content"]. The Content of this book shall not constitute or be construed or deemed to reflect the opinion or expression of the Publisher or Editor. Neither the Publisher nor Editor endorse or approve the Content of this book or guarantee the reliability, accuracy, or completeness of the Content published herein and do not make any representations or warranties of any kind, express or implied, including but not limited to the implied warranties of merchantability, fitness for a particular purpose.

The Publisher and Editor shall not be liable whatsoever...

Made with ❤ on the BookLeaf Publishing Platform
www.bookleafpub.in
www.bookleafpub.com

*To the wanderers who chase dreams, the lovers
who embrace passion, and the souls who find
solace in the beauty of the written word. This book
is for those who dare to explore the uncharted
trails of their hearts and minds, finding ecstasy in
the journey rather than the destination. Specially
dedicated to my Dadi (grandmother), this book is
for you, "Dadi."*

Acknowledgement

This book would not have been possible without the unwavering support and love of many incredible individuals. First and foremost, I want to thank my family for always believing in me and encouraging me to pursue my passion for writing. Your love and guidance have been my foundation.

To my friends and loved ones, who have walked with me through the highs and lows, thank you for your constant support. Your presence in my life has been a source of strength and inspiration, and your words of encouragement have pushed me to keep going, even when the path seemed uncertain.

Lastly, I want to express my gratitude to the readers who will embark on this journey with me. Your time and attention are precious, and I am honored to share my work with you. May these poems touch your heart and inspire you to find your own trail of ecstasy.

Preface

Trail of Ecstasy is a journey—a poetic exploration of many paths that lead us to joy, love, longing, and self-discovery. This collection is not just a series of poems but a reflection of my deepest emotions, thoughts, and experiences. Each poem is a step along a trail, winding through the landscapes of heart and soul, capturing moments of intense passion, fleeting happiness, and profound insight.

The title, *A Trail of Ecstasy*, encapsulates the essence of this collection. It's about the pursuit of that elusive feeling, the highs and lows we encounter along the way, and the beauty found in the journey itself. Poetry, for me, is the most intimate form of expression—one that allows emotions to be distilled into words, giving voice to the unspoken and form to the abstract.

As you flip through these pages, I invite you to walk with me along these trails, to experience the ecstasy of life in its myriad forms. Whether you're a seasoned traveler of poetic realms or just beginning to explore, I hope these poems resonate with you, offering comfort, inspiration, and perhaps a little bit of magic.

1. Unbound flock

In a wink of a second
She came and sat
On the top of a statue,
Little did she know
About the glimpse of civilian value.

Roving inclusively
She tried to break
Out of that space,
Sitting in a buzzed tone,
Her dynamic endeavors
Were chased.

We slur the fond of sovereignty,
That a tiny warbler
Could make
In a blink, her plume of
Feathers make a skylight
To break.

2. A Fearless Sanguine Fire

Unaware of the outside world
She was a fearless sanguine fire
From way up to modest,
No one can match her fierce desire.
Of all far n wide
She held her head up high
In the darkest of all gloom
She didn't get a single sigh.
Everything was perfect till,
They met their eyes.
Aura, she holds finally
Went into flies.
Seized all the splintered chunks
She didn't even cry.
All she longed was for him,
To get her side by.

Rushed through the hustle
To get his last glimpse.
O holy, she only got
Her tiny shrimps.
She made herself again prior
'Coz, she is a fearless sanguine fire...

3. I'll Meet You There

From softly glowing light sky
When sun equipped to meet loam
Away from the doom and gloom
When the warbler warbles in dome
Rain drizzle on the flag
When pearls of deep blue meet gravel
Like the peace of a calm runnel
When one meets its soul
I'll meet you there
When moon glances from glare
Day ends with your ring
When humming settles in spring
My heart throbs in a race
When breeze crisp on face
I'll meet you there
When trawl dances on waves
When Babe meets her Dave
I'll meet you there.

4. Let It Go

Things are not meant to be
It is not destined
It's not your fault
Things shouldn't halt
Let it go baby
Just let it go
Day will rise again
Better night will come
Let it bleed baby
Just let it cry
Don't hold your desires
Don't lose yourself
Above all again
You will shine like hell.

Keep your back straight
And your head high
What you have lost
Was never in your bag
Just let it go baby
Just let it cry
Forgive the past
Cheers right now
Moment is soon
Let it be wow
Let it go baby
Just let it go.

5. Ariel Desire

Swirling slowly in deep blue wave
Thought emerges quietly insane
Neither glare sways nor the rain
Why our world kept refrain.

Flowing from corals to red sea whip
Thoughts of the outside never got split
Only blue moon's glimpse can make it lit
This true blue impulse made me dip.

When glittery twilight hits the sky
When chilly gales don't lie
When warmth of umbra holds me tight
I want the shade of bloom near my sight

Wish I could fly high up in azure
Either my credence not sure
Fascinations that hit, made me endure
This realism keeps us obscure

Neither glare sways nor the rain
Why our world kept refrain.

6. Know Oneself

In the gallop of vicinity
In the trail of ecstasy
Lies a notion and,
A flash to know oneself.
In the loop of imagination
In the boost of hesitation
She crossed a route
To unfold a track of innovation.
From the depth of waves
To the height of caves
She clenched herself into a pave.
Gale can't tremble her,
Swells can't drench
Aura she ignites
Can't be wrenched.

In the shallow of gloom
In the sniff of bloom
Lies a notion and,
A flash to know oneself.

7. My Everything - Ma

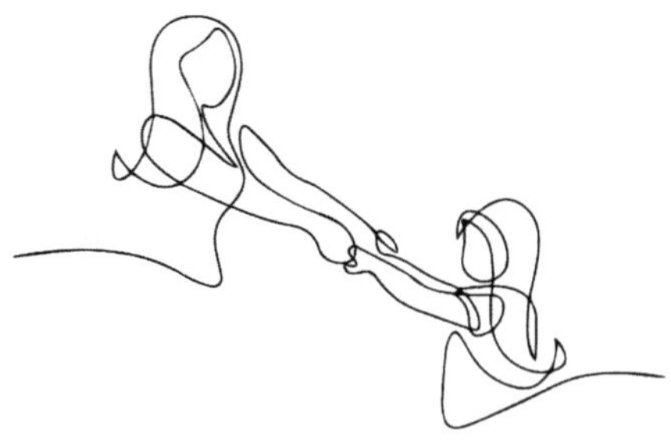

Like a shade, you hold all of us, Ma
Whatever ups n downs, right or wrong
You never left us, Ma.
Without you I'm nothing
With you I'm everything
Whatever high and low, back n forth
You never left us, Ma.

From the dim shade of diva
Staring secretly behind the wall
Glowing like a shimmering star
Like a sword in the war.

Moon on your forehead
Took all my relieve
Smile on your glowing face
Makes me believe
Came out of darkest hour
Only because of you, Ma.

Shiny chain on your wrist
All the good luck in my fist
Your hand on my forehead
Is all I have ever wished
Like a shade, you hold all of us, Ma
You hold all of us, Ma.

8. In Aroma of Books

I had an undesirable tale
Bond we shared,
Is out of veil.

Seated ideally
On the quarter of bench
Sniff of its sheet
Makes me clench.

Assembling my grip,
It made me rise.
The consort I got
Has made me wise.

As I turned out,
Its minty sheaf
Relieves the cradle
Once made its chief.

9. Just Be Happy

Don't be sad,
Just be happy
There's a lot
Just be nappy
Broken relations,
Broken friendship
Just be patient,
Overcome the hardship
Make new friends
Meet new people
Travel all round,
Move to steeple
Future is unknown,
Past is clone
Move out of that circle,
Love first own.
Life is short,
Just be snappy
Live to the best
Even if it's yappy.

10. Mirror

Standing still at the corner
Aspects of oneself
Can be seen all together.

Reality lies across me
Might be bitter
But grander apart from
Instagram filter.

One who perceived
Veraciousness of life
That indeed wins
Own life.

Shadows that reflect
Makes me feel wise
Resilience that I hold
Makes oneself rise.

Breaking all norms
Freeing from the cage
To learn and unlearn
There is no age.

11. Me And The Moon

It seems to be a strong bond,
Between me and you.
It glows differently
In the shiny sparkle of you.

Spreading deep inside,
A ray of vibes from you.
Miles of distance covered,
Easily by just a look at you.

From the shadow of veil,
I just look for the blaze of you.
Watery gaze looking up,
Wish could meet once,
Wrapping up in arms
Just wanna be there with you.

It seems to be magical,
In the light of you.
It nurtures differently,
In the crisp of you.

12. Twilight's Grace

In the quiet of twilight's grace,
Where shadows softly kiss the day,
Your laughter lingers, an endless trace,
In memories that gently sway.

The stars align in silent hymn,
Their whispers weave through evening's calm,
A canvas painted with the dim,
Yet filled with light, a soothing balm.

Stars unwind all magical wink
Place where love meets its glimpse
His voice that makes me sink
Emotions in the core, are like blimps.

Our hearts entwine in tender verse,
A melody both sweet and clear,
With every line, the world immerses,
In the love that we hold dear.

13. I Wanna Be With You

In the shade of moon
In the glimpse of bloom
I just wanna be with you.

In the pearls of rain
In the crust of vain
I just wanna be the clout of you.

Wherever I go, whenever I see
I grasped you, embraced you.
From deep core
To the last breath
From first sight
To the last death
I just wanna feel you.

May all your sorrow rest on my wink
I waited for you without a blink
How can I tell what you mean
You hold my heart like a shin.

14. Nature's Echoes

In the whisper of leaves, a quiet melody holds
Healing all the wrath, something it unfolds.

The river sang a soothing tune,
Mountain echoes its ancient croons,
Nature is orchestra, a symphony untold.

Rain taps softly on the window
Birds' chirps are like a mellow.
Gravel beneath the feet, feels like a soft
feather
Like paradise on Earth, is such a weather.

Minty Dew on the green
Walking bare feet, makes me feel like a teen.
Cold wind binds me in like a blow
Truly met oneself once in a lifetime though.

In the whisper of leaves, a quiet melody holds
Feeling one's soul, something it molds...

15. Eclipsed By Stars

Under twilight's veil, where secrets hide,
There's a world unseen, where echoes play,
A dance of whispers in the break of day.

In moments still, where silence speaks,
Find strength in the calm, where solace leaks.
Stars align with path untold,
A journey in your soul, both fierce and bold.

Your heart's compass, true and bright,
Guiding through the stars toward the light.
With every step, your spirit sings,
A melody that Universe brings.

No shadow lingers in your wake,
Just a trail of stardust in its wake.
So when the night feels deep and long,
Remember within you, lies a song.

16. Unrequited Love

Looking up at him, with sparkling cheering eyes.
Wish I could tell, how much his notion made me cry.
Falling a little bit more, each and every day
Wished, I would confess to him, one day.

One sight of him, cages all my grace
Silence he holds, made me lose my pace.
Now I'm not with me, every heartbeat rests with his sleep.
His misery and bliss, are all I want to keep.

His black dazzling gaze, longing for fire
Butterflies I get, shaking all my desires.
Above all diffusion of dusky sky,
When Sun meets its twilight,
Melodious saga unite us, every night.

One day, when pearl shines from waves,
When all sorrow, hides in caves
Walking barefoot on shimmery sand,
Souls will meet, when hands in hand.
Melody sprinkles all round, by dove
Glistening eyes show, all mine love.

17. Unfinished

Under serene dawn, in the dark woods,
Where gaze of the moon, covering the hoods.
Met him first time, just to know,
Little did I know, he would be my beau.

Slowly yet surely, every ounce of my core, he
stole
Little did I know, I met a purest soul.
Endless talks, makes my heart melt
Like a divine princess, he made me felt.

As the darkest hour filled the sky,
Promises we made, turned into a lie.
Something crushing inside, made me felt
Universe turned upside down, heart grieved
and melt.

Society parted us, liabilities distanced
Hanged till ultimate hour, with fierce
persistence.
With warmth in core, treasure in gaze
Soul sprinkled the love, defeated by fate.

Like a euphoric chant, a warbler vague when,
Mine glance longed, core raced of him then.
Mesmerizing glorious hazel gaze, what I last
wish,
Hope beyond the discover, till eternity, our
souls will kiss.

18. Divine Sky

The sky unfolds in shades of blue,
A canvas vast, forever new,
It whispers softly, calls your name,
In every breath, it speaks the same.

The clouds like dreams drift far away,
Painting the hopes of yesterday,
While sunbeams dance upon your face,
And time stands still in their embrace.

The stars will rise when day is done,
To guide you 'til the morning sun,
And in their glow, you'll find the way,
To chase your dreams through night and day.

So trust the winds that kiss the sea,
And let your heart forever be
A vessel full of love and light,
To sail the endless, starry night.

19. Flaunt Yourself

It's beautiful to give wings to your
imagination,
It's okay not to reach up to destination.

Let your desire be reborn again,
Let the scar move out of pain.

Slowly, slowly craft a new masterpiece,
Hold the moment and let it freeze.

As the fresh gale move towards the casement,
Your inner flaunts got a new replacement.

It's beautiful to burn all your doubts into
ashes,
It's okay to enlighten oneself with new flashes.

Hold the whistle, remove the scar,
The day you outshine, is not so far.

Chimes of triumph, are all you hear,
Step out of that zone, everything will be near.
It's beautiful to give wings to your
imagination,
It's okay not to reach up to destination.

Let your desire be reborn again,
Let the scar move out of pain.

Slowly, slowly craft a new masterpiece,
Hold the moment and let it freeze.

As the fresh gale move towards the casement,

Your inner flaunts got a new replacement.

It's beautiful to burn all your doubts into
ashes,
It's okay to enlighten oneself with new flashes.

Hold the whistle, remove the scar,
The day you outshine, is not so far.

Chimes of triumph, are all you hear,
Move out of that zone, everything will be
near.

20. Waves of Time

The ocean sings with ancient waves,
A rhythm carved in secret caves,
Each ripple tells a tale untold,
Of memories both young and old.

The tides that rise, the tides that fall,
They whisper stories, one and all,
Of fleeting days and moments lost,
Of hearts that sailed but paid the cost.

Yet in the foam, new hopes are born,
With every breaking wave at dawn,
And though the past drifts far behind,
The sea of time is always kind.

For every wave that leaves the shore,
Another brings us something more:
A chance to love, a chance to find,
The treasure left for heart and mind.

21. When Heart Calls Out

Love is when,
It does mystic wonders to you
One word brings happiness anew.
His eyes sweep away all your sorrows
That much divine, a smile can borrow.

Love occurs,
When soul reaches its peace.
Even the worst scene, feels like Greece.
When world hits you more down,
He offers you an alluring crown.

Love feels,
Like a flying flick, on a wave.
Enlightened pearl resting in a nave.
Like the greatest feeling, an experience, a
dream,
It holds emotions, drama, fun and gleam.

May the greatest love stories lie on your door,
Go out and explore, find one for your
folklore.

www.ingramcontent.com/pod-product-compliance
Lightning Source LLC
LaVergne TN
LVHW050942200726

843508LV00011B/2421